James L. Gleason

A publication of Sonrise Church, Hillsboro, OR

© 2014 by James L. Gleason

Published by Sonrise Church
6701 NE Campus Way, Hillsboro, OR 97124-5500
www.isonrise.com

ISBN 978-1514227572

All rights reserved. No part of this publication may be reproduced, stored in a retrieval system, or transmitted in any form or by any means–for example, electronic, photocopy, recording–without the prior written permission of the publisher.

Scripture quotations are taken from the Holy Bible, New Living Translation, copyright ©1996, 2004, 2007, 2013 by Tyndale House Foundation. Used by permission of Tyndale House Publishers, Inc., Carol Stream, Illinois 60188. All rights reserved.

Cover design and interior graphics by Annette Sabo Brooks

INTRODUCTION

Congratulations! Taking the step of faith to follow Jesus Christ is the greatest single step you will ever take. Like any journey, this one step will lead you to many more steps. One day your steps will lead you right into the arms of the one who loved you enough to die for you.

In John 10:10 Jesus said,

> *The thief's purpose is to steal and kill and destroy. My purpose is to give them a rich and satisfying life.*

You are probably deeply aware of how much the thief (Satan) has stolen, killed, and tried to destroy your life. Your new "rich and satisfying life" began the moment you stepped over the line of faith and decided to follow Jesus. But this is just the beginning of experiencing your new life. What do I do now?

That is the purpose of this little book. Over the next four weeks I want to introduce you to the storyline of God and where you fit into God's story.

Have you ever stopped to notice that all inspiring movies speak through the storyline of *Creation, Fall, Redemption,* and *Restoration*? As I write this I have just returned from training pastors in Africa and the long flights allowed me to catch up on popular movies I have missed. I was reminded once again of this storyline pattern as each movie followed the same pattern: a hopeful beginning, a tragic accident, a great struggle to reclaim, and hopefully, a final reinstatement that culminated in a just and happy ending. This pattern of *Creation, Fall, Redemption,* and *Restoration* was in every movie I watched.

Last summer my family and I were given a special invitation to visit PIXAR Studios–home of Toy Story and other animated children's movies. PIXAR is known for having compelling animation, but what really sets them apart from other movie companies is their attention to the art of storytelling.

Consider the storyline of *Creation*, *Fall*, *Redemption*, and *Restoration* in light of PIXAR's films: In Toy Story we see *Creation* when Woody (a toy cowboy) and Andy (the child) have a wonderful life playing together in Andy's room. All of this is interrupted when Buz (a new toy spaceman) interrupts this peaceful life. The *Fall* occurs as Woody gets he and Buz hopelessly lost. The rest of the movie works through the process of *Redemption* when Woody discovers he is loved and valued in spite of this new toy that threatened to take Andy's affections. It is only in the last few minutes that *Restoration* occurs and everyone finds their way home.

Finding Nemo is another example of this proven storyline working itself out in the drama of film. We see *Creation* when two clown fish named Marlin and Coral create their home on the Great Barrier Reef and have their babies. The *Fall* happens within moments when a shark attacks their home. Coral and all but one egg are eaten. Marlin raises his only son, Nemo, until he is captured by a diver and taken to Sydney. The theme of *Redemption* takes the rest of the movie as Marlin searches the ocean depths to find his son. The final movement reveals the *Restoration* of Marlin and Nemo–together safe once again. Every PIXAR movie follows this same storyline.

We can see this storyline flow through the greatest stories of our age– from Ben Hur to It's a Wonderful Life, from the Godfather to the Gladiator, from the Wizard of Oz to E.T. the Extra-Terrestrial. Why does this storyline grab our attention and wrap us up in its drama? I believe it is because they all echo the storyline of our own existence: a story of *Creation*, *Fall*, *Redemption*, and *Restoration*. This is our story.

Over the next four weeks we will be looking at the greatest story of all and discovering that God has a part in the story for you.

– *Pastor James Gleason*

STORYLINES

Introduction 1

Week 1: Creation 4
    Day 1. Creator
    Day 2. Beginning
    Day 3. Creation
    Day 4. Image
    Day 5. Rest

Week 2: Fall 14
    Day 1. Relationship
    Day 2. Temptation
    Day 3. Rebellion
    Day 4. Consequences
    Day 5. Death

Week 3: Redemption 24
    Day 1. Bankrupt
    Day 2. Redeemer
    Day 3. Sacrifice
    Day 4. Resurrection
    Day 5. Relationship

Week 4: Restoration 34
    Day 1. Hope
    Day 2. Rebuilding
    Day 3. Judgment
    Day 4. Justice
    Day 5. Heaven

Conclusion 44

Day 1: Creator

Have you ever had one of those moments where you looked up at the night sky or stood looking at a sunset and knew you were not alone? Have you ever wondered where everything came from and what we are doing here?

Humanity has always seen something bigger than themselves when they looked at the creation all around them. The shear magnitude of the world we live in causes us to consider where it came from. Was it an accident? Was it mere chance? Was it designed? If so, by whom?

In the Bible we find a clear picture of a God who is both creator and friend. Most importantly, we discover a God who wants to know us and be in a relationship with us.

This first week of our **Storyline** we will discover **Creation** and how our Creator originally planned for our world to be.

Read Romans 1:19-20. How can we know about God?

> By going to church, reading the Bible and speaking to the church community/ people who know about God.

Read Psalm 90:2. How long has God been around?

> God has been around since the beginning. He is the Creator of everything.

Read Jeremiah 9:23-24. How can this God be known?

> God has given us all of what we have. We should not brag of what we have/he has given us or he can take it away.

Read Psalm 139:7-10. How does God's presence affect your thoughts of him?

God is everywhere. Hence, if I believe in him and have faith he will always be beside me. So, I should not do things that are against God and what he stands for.

Read Jeremiah 32:17. How does God's power affect your view of your circumstances?

God has a plan. I can be happy with whatever little or too much I have or I can be happy with what little or too much I have with God alongside me.

Read 1 John 3:20. How does God's knowledge affect your view of yourself?

I do not hate the light. I have liked the light and until recently I have learned to like the light even more with getting to know God.

Application & Reflection

What did you learn today?

All who do evil hate the light and refuse to go near it for fear their sins will be exposed.

How will it affect you?

I will try to continue to learn how to love the light so I can be a role model and use it to make disciples one day.

Storylines: Discover Your Part in the Story

CREATION

Day 2: Beginning

Perhaps the most profound words in the Bible are its very first words. In Genesis 1:1 we read, "In the beginning God created the heavens and the earth." In this short statement the foundation is laid for everything we see around us and know inside us. This simply lays the foundation of the rest of the Bible.

The lifelong questions of "where did I come from?", "why am I here?", and "what is my purpose in life?" are all answered as we understand that everything we see began because God chose to create our very existence.

Read Genesis 1:1. Share your thoughts on the following words:

• *Beginning*: The very word signifies the *first*. It is used many times in the Old Testament to identify the very *first* of something. This means that Genesis 1:1 is describing the absolute beginning of our created world. What comes to your mind with this word?

The beginning of existence. In Scientific words the "Big Bang." Nothing is before that, only GOD.

• *God*: The name for God here is *Elohim* and is a general name for God in the Old Testament. *Elohim* emphasizes his greatness and power over everything and everyone. This means that God is the ultimate ruler of his creation. What comes to your mind with this word?

There is nothing/no one above him. He is the creator so he is the most powerful. Nobody can compare to GOD.

• *Created*: The Hebrew word *created* (bara) implies that God created everything out of nothing. He did not refashion previous material in his creation, but spoke everything into existence as a new creation. What comes to your mind with this word?

He created everything of nothing. He did not practice or do a Rough Draft. He must have done that on purpose.

- *Heavens*: When the Bible writers use the word *heavens*, they are referring to anything that is above us–that which is "up there." Sometimes it is used of the sky, the planets and stars, and sometimes it is used of the very place where God dwells. What comes to your mind with this word?

We tend to look up at the sky. But it also pictures the wilderness with animals and rivers where we can be in nature in harmony with the children of GOD.

- *Earth*: In contrast to the starry heavens, the *earth* is what is "down here" and is our domain. The earth is the soil of our existence–and becomes the element in which God creates mankind. What comes to your mind with this word?

Where we live our human lives. Where we are happy and sad, suffer and enjoy our time here. Where our actions will someday get judged by GOD + determine if we go to heaven or not.

Application & Reflection

What did you learn today?

I determine on how I see and live my life. And I want to live my life as happy as possible and not focus on any negative thoughts.

How will it affect you?

Trying to focus on the positive side of things and live as happy as I can. Trying to remember this every time I get negative thoughts.

Day 3: Creation

Genesis 1:1-31 lays out the order of God's creation over the course of six individual days. There is an order to God's creation and a purpose to everything he creates.

The creation account is not only divided into six days, but is divided according to the location of what is created. The first three days cover the creation of the various realms and then the second three days cover the creation of the various rulers who will occupy those realms. Read the following verses and note anything that stands out to you about their creation.

God created the *Realms*:

Day 1) Light. *Read Genesis 1:2-5.*
Where did the light come from? From him/GOD?

Day 2) Sky and oceans. *Read Genesis 1:6-8.*
Seperating the waters from earth from the waters of heaven.

Day 3) Dry land. *Read Genesis 1:9-13.*
Amazing how he made plants & fruit. And having the fruit/vegetation have seeds.

God created the *Rulers*:

Day 4) Sun, moon, and stars. *Read Genesis 1:14-19.*
Amazing how he thought of making two lights. Even having light in darkness with the moon.

Day 5) Birds and fish. *Read Genesis 1:20-23.*
First he made creatures for the sky & sea.

Day 6) Animals and people. *Read Genesis 1:24-31.*

Why didn't God make animals on the 5th day? Maybe separating by realms. Mind blowing how he made us of his own image.

Read Psalm 89:11. What does this tell us about God's creation?

That everything belongs to him. And he can do whatever he decides to do and/or take it away

How does Genesis 1 challenge the prevailing world-view of our modern times?

How we are slowly destroying things GOD created.

Application & Reflection

What did you learn today?

There is an order to GOD's creation and a purpose to everything he creates.

How will it affect you?

GOD does things for a reason. I will try an accept all the hard times as much as the happier times.

Storylines: Discover Your Part in the Story

Day 4: Image

At the height of God's creation he chose to create mankind out of the dust of the earth. This final act of creation was special and a unique statement is made about men and women. In Genesis 1:27 it is said that we were created "in God's own image." Theologians call this the *imago dei* (image of God) and help us understand why God said "it is good" after every other created act, but said, "it is very good" after creating us. We were created on the last day–as the culmination of God's creation plan. We are the conclusion of creation.

It is this image of God, stamped on our lives that sets us apart from the rest of creation. We bear in our existence a special connection to our Creator. Since God does not have a spirit and does not have a physical form, this likeness is a spiritual and moral likeness. We can know God because we are made in his likeness.

Mankind's **Relationship** with God:

Read Genesis 2:7. How did mankind come into existence?

By God forming us from the dust of the earth and breathing into Adam's nostrils and then he became a living person.

Read Matthew 19:4. How do Jesus' words affirm God's unique creation of mankind?

Affirms that God made us Male and female since the beginning.

Mankind's **Responsibility** before God:

Read Genesis 1:26. What are we called to do for God's creation?

Reign over the fish in the Sea, the birds in the sky, the livestock, wild animals and all the small animals

Read Psalm 86-7. How are we to exercise authority over God's creation?

☆

Read Isaiah 43:7. Why did God make us? How does this shape our purpose in life?

God made us for his glory. By following him only then will we know what our purpose in life is.

Application & Reflection

What did you learn today?

That God has no spirit or physical form.

How will it affect you?

I will ask pastor James what this means.

Storylines: Discover Your Part in the Story

Day 5: Rest

Creation concludes with God being satisfied with all that he created. Genesis 2:1-3 states,

> *So the creation of the heavens and the earth and everything in them was completed. On the seventh day God had finished his work of creation, so he rested from all his work. And God blessed the seventh day and declared it holy, because it was the day when he rested from all his work of creation.*

It is significant that God chose to set aside the seventh day as a day to remember his rest from the work of creation. God was so serious about this rest that he declared the day *holy*–set aside for his purpose. This day is called the Sabbath.

We often think of the word rest and think *sleep*, but the creation story is not about God being tired from all that he had done and needing to take a break! The Hebrew word means to *cease from activity*. God was finished with his work and very satisfied—so he stopped working. From the very beginning of creation God has built in a weekly calendar of six days of work and one day of rest.

According to Jewish tradition, "one should avoid one's normal occupation or profession on the Sabbath whenever possible and engage only in those types of activities that enhance the joy, rest, and holiness of the day."

Read Exodus 20:8. What did God declare about the seventh day?

Observe the Sabbath day by keeping it Holy.

Read Mark 2:27-28. According to Jesus why was the Sabbath created?

To meet the needs of people.

How can you build in the discipline to honor God by learning to rest one day a week. What steps will you take to focus on those things that bring you joy, rest, and draw you closer to God and his people?

By finishing this book. By going to church/service on Sundays. Possibly doing a bit more on Sundays in regards to reading bible/spending time with family which brings joy.

Application & Reflection

What did you learn today?

That the Sabbath is to do activities that enhance joy, rest, and holiness of the day.

How will it affect you?

I will try to do activities that enhance joy, rest, and holiness. Start by reading the bible for 30 min on Sunday and spending family time.

Conclusion of Week 1: Creation

Sum up the story of God's creation: Our creator who has existed since the beginning of time. God created the earth in 6 days and on the seventh day he rested and made it holy and named it the Sabbath. God made us in his own image and we are to reign over all the animals/creatures on earth.

Storylines: Discover Your Part in the Story

Day 1: Relationship

Have you ever had one of those perfect relationships where every moment was filled with perfect communication and unending joy? If the answer is "no," then you're in good company. No one since Adam and Eve has experienced this kind of peace and intimacy in any relationship.

What was once intended to be pure would quickly become corrupted. What was once intended to last forever would quickly end with God banishing Adam and Eve from Eden.

God had designed mankind in his image to enjoy an ongoing relationship with Adam, Eve, and their descendants. Imagine the perfect relationship of complete transparency and love.

This second week of our **Storyline** we will discover the *Fall* of mankind and how we destroyed this perfect relationship.

Read Genesis 2:25. What was special about Adam and Eve's relationship with each other?

They felt no shame. They were transparent.

Read Genesis 3:8. This verse describes a regular encounter with God where he would come down to walk and talk with Adam and Eve. What does this tells us about how they knew God and related to him?

Read Genesis 2:15. What job did God give to Adam?

To tend and watch over the

garden of Eden.

Read Genesis 2:16. What was the "yes" God told to Adam?

He could eat fruit from every tree in the garden.

Read Genesis 2:17. What was the only "no"?

Except from the tree of knowledge of good and evil.

Read Genesis 2:17. What would be the result of disobedience?

If he ate the fruit he will die.

Application & Reflection

What did you learn today?

God gives us the freedom to do whatever we want. However, there are things he doesn't want us doing which will have consequences.

How will it affect you?

Not just because I'm free to do what I want I should. Think twice before doing something and ask myself if I'm disobeying God.

Day 2: Temptation

The temptation that Adam and Eve faced is no different from what you and I encounter today–except for the fact that they could have said "no" and walked away from the temptation. Our lives are tainted with inner sinful desires and Adam and Eve had not yet known this built-in temptation.

Many Bible experts believe that if Adam and Eve would have responded properly to this one temptation, then God would have removed the temptation and they could have lived forever in a perfect condition of purity with him. The love they shared with God had to be tested. They had to be given a choice to obey or disobey God. True love is always a decision and can never be forced or coerced.

Unfortunately, this temptation proved too difficult to resist and you and I suffer from their one decision to rebel against God. We can learn a lot about our own temptations to sin by looking at their temptation and response.

Read Genesis 3:1-7. How did the serpent (Satan in disguise) tempt Adam and Eve?

> By telling them that they would be like God, knowing both good and evil as soon as they ate it.

Read James 1:13-15. How do you see the temptation process working its way out in Adam and Eve's temptation?

> By the tree being the most colorful/prettiest with the best looking fruit. Also it being forbidden. And what it would do after eating it as the snake says.

Read 1 John 2:15-17. In verse 16 John describes three desires that plunge us into sin. What are they?
- A desire for __pleasure__
- A desire for __Greed__
- A desire for __Pride__

Read Genesis 3:6. How did Eve face these same three desires?
- Pleasure __of eating the delicious looking fruit.__
- Greed __of gaining the wisdom it would give her.__
- Pride __of eating the fruit first before Adam.__

How do you see these same three desires draw you towards temptation?
- Pleasure __of being with other woman__
- Greed __of making more money than I need__
- Pride __of being better than everyone else.__

Application & Reflection

What did you learn today?

__The 3 desires that push us into sin: pleasure, Greed and Pride.__

How will it affect you?

__Try to think and ask myself about the situation at hand if it's being affected by one of the three desires.__

Storylines: Discover Your Part in the Story

Day 3: Rebellion

Genesis 1-2 describes a perfect world with perfect people in a perfect relationship with a perfect God. Sadly, it all came to a crashing halt when Adam and Eve rebelled against God.

The idea to sin came to Eve through Satan. It was Satan's first sin that had expelled him from the presence of God (see Ezekiel 28:11-17 and Isaiah 14:12-14) and he sought the same for Adam and Eve. All he had to do was to cause them to doubt the goodness of God. His lies about God's motives, what God had actually said, and the fact the fruit was forbidden caused Eve to reach out and take a bite. She then handed it to Adam who was standing beside her and he had his bite.

It was God's intention for Adam and Eve to remain in a pure, innocent state, but sadly this could not happen now that they had disobeyed God and eaten the forbidden fruit. Although Eve was the one deceived, it was Adam who was held responsible for their actions.

Read Genesis 3:6-7. What was Adam and Eve's response to the only prohibition that God had given to them?

They disobeyed and ate the forbidden fruit.

Read 1 Timothy 2:13-14. How does Paul describe the chain of events in Genesis 3?

If we are unfaithful, he will remain faithful for that is who he is. Also to not fight over words. Arguments/words can ruin those who hear them.

Read Romans 5:12. What consequence has everyone suffered because of Adam's one sin?

Adams sin brought death.

Read 1 John 1:8-10. What does this tell us about our condition before God?

That people didn't recognize him.

Read Romans 3:23. What is the result of Adam & Eve's sin against God?

Made everyone sinners.

Application & Reflection

What did you learn today?

That we are all sinners from the day we are born.

How will it affect you?

So if we are sinners when we are born, when is it the best time to get baptized? Baby or Adult?

Storylines: Discover Your Part in the Story

Day 4: Consequences

As soon as Adam and Eve sinned and came to the knowledge of good and evil they were aware of their own nakedness. This shame led them to hastily put together a covering of fig leaves, run from God when he came looking for them, and then attempt to hide from his presence. Once confronted on their sin they chose to blame everyone else for their actions and refused to confess their guilt before God.

Isn't that how it works in our lives too? When we sin, our shame and guilt causes us to cover up our sin, go into hiding, and deny the destructive impact sin has had on our lives. Once caught, we blame anyone or anything instead of admitting our guilt and need for God's grace.

The result of their sin was a series of curses that will haunt us until the day God recreates everything to its original state. In his mercy, God covered Adam and Eve with the skin of animals and sent them out of the Garden of Eden. Even this was an act of grace. After all, God did not want them to eat of the Tree of Life and live forever in their broken condition.

Read Genesis 3:8-9. Why do you think God called out to Adam asking him where he was?

> To see if he would lie about where he was.

Read Genesis 3:10-11. What do you think was the significance of Adam and Eve being naked and ashamed?

Read Genesis 3:12-13. Once caught, who did Adam and Eve blame for their sin?
- Adam blamed __eve__
- Eve blamed __the serpent__

Read Genesis 3:14-19. How were the various players in this act of the *Storyline* cursed?
- The serpent (14) __will crawl on his belly__
- The devil (15) __hostility between woman + humans + "it"__
- Eve (16) __pain during pregnancy/birth & husband rule over her__
- Adam (17-18) __to struggle to make a living__
- Creation (19) __by labor/working we will earn food to eat until we die.__

We are all free to choose our actions, but choices and results are inseparable. Even though we hide because of our shame and guilt, God seeks us out and covers us with his love.

Application & Reflection

What did you learn today?
__The ways the various players got cursed.__

How will it affect you?
__We were cursed to work until we die to make a living. But will look at it not as a curse but as a must as we are here to earn our food.__

Day 5: Death

Adam and Eve now realized the extent of their rebellion against God. As they fled the Garden of Eden their spiritual condition was now broken beyond their own repair. Eve would suffer pain in childbirth, Adam would work by the sweat of his brow, and the earth would fight them as they sought to rule over it. Everything was broken.

This was far more than they bargained for and the impact of their sin was beyond just knowing good and evil–they actually became evil. Their hearts and minds became darkened and were unable to fellowship with God as they had before.

The word for death in the Bible carries with it the idea of *separation*. When we die physically our bodies die and our immaterial state goes on to judgment. Our spiritual death comes through birth because we are all in the line of Adam. We are spiritually separated from God and cannot repair the damage.

Adam and Eve's one sin altered the course of human history and brought death to all their descendants.

Read 1 Corinthians 15:56. What is the sting of sin?

<u>For sin is the sting that results in death, and the law gives sin its power</u>

Read Romans 6:23. How has sin affected us?

<u>The wages of sin equal death separation from God.</u>

Read Romans 5:12. How far has Adam's sin spread?

It has spread to everyone on this earth.

Read 2 Corinthians 4:4. What has Satan done to people because they are separated from God?

Blinded the minds of those who don't believe about the glory of Christ.

Application & Reflection

What did you learn today?

That I'm being blinded when I don't read the bible, follow Jesus Christ.

How will it affect you?

I would like to slowly start opening my eyes and start to get to know the glory of God.

Conclusion of Week 2: Fall

Sum up the story of mankind's fall from grace:

It all started with Adam and Eve. Everything was good until they disobeyed God and ate the forbidden fruit. Due to their sin they have caused and brought death to everyone on Earth.

Day 1: Bankrupt

When Adam and Eve sinned and fell from innocence, they condemned not only themselves but all of their descendants to spiritual separation from God. There is nothing we can do to repair the situation because we are spiritually helpless and morally bankrupt. Even our good works are useless to win back God's favor and clear the record of our sins. The only hope we have is for God to reach down and pay our spiritual debt and restore what we have broken.

This third week of our **Storyline** we will discover the **Redemption** God offers to us and his method of bringing us back into a right relationship with him.

Read Isaiah 64:6. What does God say about our spiritual condition? Will our good works help us reach out to God?

> Our righteous deeds are nothing but filthy rags. No, our sin sweeps us away.

Read Romans 3:10-12. What does this passage tell us about our ability to reach out to God on our own effort?

> We all have turned away. No one is seeking God on our own.

Read Isaiah 59:2. Why are we separated from God?

> Our sins have separates us from God.

Read Colossians 1:21. How does God view us in our broken, sinful condition? What causes our separation from God?

> He views us as his enemies. Our evil thoughts and actions separate us from God.

Read Revelation 20:11-12. In a very somber tone, this passage in Revelation describes the painful end of all those who do not know God. At this Great White Throne judgment, how will people be judged?

> The dead were judged according to what they had done, as recorded in the books.

Read Revelation 20:13-15. What is the painful end to those who have not received eternal life through Jesus Christ?

> They will be thrown into the lake of fire.

Application & Reflection

What did you learn today?

> That God views us as his enemy.

How will it affect you?

> Try to take control of my thoughts and actions so they are good and not evil. This will be hard but I have to try.

Day 2: Redeemer

In the Bible, the word *redeem* means "to buy back from bondage" and "to ransom persons or property that had been sold for a debt." That is an excellent picture of what God did for us in sending Jesus Christ to pay the penalty for our sin.

Because of our sinful condition we have all been sold into slavery to sin and have no way of purchasing our freedom. We need a redeemer to come and rescue us from our bondage. Thankfully, God has chosen to pay the price to buy us back.

Read Isaiah 53:6. How have we lived our lives and how did God step in to rescue us?

Like sheep and have strayed away. Left God's path to follow our own. Jesus dying for us and our sins.

Read John 3:16-17. How did God take the initiative to rescue us when we all deserve judgment and death? What does God ask in return?

He loved the world so much he gave his one and only son. He asks for us to believe in his son, so we can have eternal life.

Read Galatians 3:22. How does this verse say we gain freedom from our sins?

We recieve God's promise of freedom only by believing in Jesus Christ.

Read Romans 5:6-8. What does this passage tell us about how God works on our behalf to redeem us?

God showed his great love for us as he sent Christ to die for us even though we were all sinners.

Read Ephesians 2:8-9. Can we earn this salvation? If not, how do we receive it? Does this matter?

Salvation is not a reward, it is a gift from God by his grace when we believe in Jesus. It matters because we can not take credit for this and or boast about it.

Read Romans 6:23. According to this verse, what does our sin earn and what does God's gift give us instead?

the wages of sin is death, God gives us eternal life through Jesus Christ.

Application & Reflection

What did you learn today?

That Salvation is a gift from God and we recieve it only by believing in Jesus Christ.

How will it affect you?

Believing that not just by doing good deeds and being good you will be saved. It takes for you to believe in Jesus Christ for those good deeds to matter.

Day 3: Sacrifice

In Genesis 3:21 we read that after Adam and Eve had sinned and tried to cover themselves with leaves, God stepped in and made real clothing from animal skins. This act led to the first occasion where innocent blood had to be spilled to adequately cover sin. In God's plan for our salvation a sacrifice is required to cover sin. In the Bible, the word *atone* means to "cover," "blot out," or "remove guilt."

In the Old Testament God laid out a system of atoning sacrifices so the people's sins could be covered over year after year. These sacrifices all required the death of an pure and spotless animal. This animal became the substitute for the people's own sin.

As the New Testament opens, the concept of a sacrifice was finally understood when Jesus died on the cross. He died our death. His blood covered our sin. Jesus was our perfect spotless sacrificial substitution.

Read Hebrews 9:22. What does forgiveness require?

The shedding of blood.

Read 1 John 2:2. What did Jesus become for us?

He became the sacrifice (for the sins of all the world).

Read 2 Corinthians 5:21. How does Paul describe what Jesus did on our behalf?

He was an offering for our sin, so that we could be made right with God through him (Jesus).

Read Hebrews 9:28. How does the writer of Hebrews describe what Jesus did on our behalf?

> That Jesus was sacrificed to take away our sins (the sins of many people).

Read 1 Peter 2:24. How does Peter describe what Jesus did on our behalf?

> Jesus carried our sins in his body on the cross. By his wounds we are healed.

Read Isaiah 53:1-12. Write down all the ways these words were ultimately fulfilled in Jesus:

_____

_____

_____

Read Matthew 27:1-66 and consider Christ dying for you.

Application & Reflection

What did you learn today?

> That forgiveness requires the shedding of blood. And that Jesus carried our sins in his body on the cross. By his wounds we are healed.

How will it affect you?

> I never looked at it in the way Peter describes Jesus' sacrifice. I only knew it as he died for us.

Day 4: Resurrection

Why did Jesus die? To pay the price for our sinfulness and bring us back to God. Why did Jesus rise again? To prove our faith in Christ is real and to give us hope for our own eventual resurrection. The Apostle Paul wrote in 1 Corinthians 15:17,

> *If Christ has not been raised, then your faith is useless and you are still guilty of your sins.*

The resurrection of Christ was not an afterthought but the culmination of the sacrifice Jesus made for us. When he rose again he demonstrated his own power over the grave. It is an essential part of our story of forgiveness.

Read the story of Christ's resurrection in John 20:1-31.

Read 1 Corinthians 15:3-23. Note the significance of what the Apostle Paul wrote:

- (3) Christ died for our sins
- (4) Christ rose from the dead.
- (5) He was seen by the disciples
- (6) Seen by more than 500 followers at one time
- (7) Seen by James and later by all the apostles
- (8) Paul also saw him
- (9) Paul believes he is the least of the apostles
- (13) believe in resurrection
- (14) preaching would be useless without resurrection
- (15) apostles would be lying about Christ's resurrection
- (16) Christ has not been raised if resurrection is a lie
- (17) still guilty of our sins without resurrection

- (18) Dead believing in Christ are lost
- (19) hope in Christ for more than this life
- (20) Christ is the first of a great harvest
- (21) death because of Adam, resurrection because of Jesus
- (22) believers in Christ will be given new life
- (23) all who belong to Christ will be raised when he comes back

Read John 11:25. Why does the resurrection matter?

Anyone who believes in Jesus will live after dying. Part of God's plan.

Read Acts 2:32 & Acts 17:31. In both Peter and Paul's messages, the key is the resurrection of Jesus from the grave. Why is this essential to the Good News about Jesus?

Gives us hope & faith

Application & Reflection

What did you learn today?

That Jesus resurrected to prove our faith in Christ is real and to give us hope for our own eventual resurrection.

How will it affect you?

It will give me the knowledge & wisdom to be able to share with others

Day 5: Relationship

It's really amazing when you stop and think about it. God created us for a relationship with him, and even when we rebelled and pursued our own interests, he reached out to invite us back. Our rebellion had significant consequences that we were unable to fix, so God came in and took care of the situation and paid the debt for us. It was a steep price, but for some reason his love overcame all costs. Now that the debt has been paid God invites us to rejoin the relationship. Why would anyone say, "no" to such a generous offer?

Unfortunately we have grown accustomed to being in charge of our lives and the thought of giving that up is too much for many people. Will we humble ourselves and pursue the only one who can rescue us from our broken condition?

Read 1 John 4:10. How has God pursued us?

By showing us he loves us and even sending his one and only son as a sacrifice to clear our sins.

Read Acts 17:27. How far away is God?

He is not far from anyone of us.

Read Isaiah 53:6. How have we acted towards God and how did he respond to our need?

We have strayed away and follow our own path. Yet God laid all the sins of everyone on Jesus as he was sacrificed.

Read 1 Peter 3:18. What is God's solution for our sin?

To sacrifice Jesus to save us so we can come home to him.

Read Titus 3:3-7. Can our own efforts fix our brokenness?

No, it was by God's grace and mercy.

Read John 1:12. How do we become a child of God?

By believing and accepting Jesus Christ.

Application

Have you believed and received Jesus Christ as Savior and Lord? If not, you may find it helpful to express yourself to God with words such as these:

> Dear God, I know that my sin has separated me from you. Thank you for sending Jesus Christ, to die in my place. I now trust Jesus to forgive my sins. I choose to follow him as my Savior and Lord. Thank you for receiving me into your eternal family. In Jesus' name, amen.

Conclusion of Week 3: Redemption

Sum up the story of Jesus' work on the cross on own behalf:

Sin separated us from God so he viewed us as his enemy. Thus God sent his only son Jesus as a sacrifice to die for our sin so we can be redeemed. Then Jesus resurrected to give us hope & faith. He wants a relationship with us for he loves us.

Storylines: Discover Your Part in the Story

Day 1: Hope

One of the greatest lines from our children's stories offers such hope: "And they lived happily ever after." This longing for a happily ever is no accident, it has has been placed their by God. Solomon wrote in Ecclesiastes 3:11,

> Yet God has made everything beautiful for its own time. He has planted eternity in the human heart, but even so, people cannot see the whole scope of God's work from beginning to end.

Every story we tell is our attempt to put into words and images what God has planted in our heart–the restoration of all things.

This fourth and last week of our **Storyline** we will discover the **Restoration** God brings when we align our lives with his will.

Read Ephesians 2:1-3. What causes all of the brokenness we encounter in our lives?

The passionate desires and inclinations of our sinful nature.

Read Ephesians 2:4-9. What did God do for us?

God gave us life when he raised Jesus Christ from the dead. God saved us by his grace when we believed.

Read Ephesians 2:10. What is God's plan for us?

For us to do the good things he planned for us long ago.

Read Hosea 6:1-3. What is the goal of God's restoration?

So that we may live in his presence.

Read Joel 2:25-26. Our sin destroys, but God restores our lives. What are you needing God to restore in your life?

The Health and love of my family as well as mine.

Read John 10:10. Satan destroys, but Jesus restores. What would a rich and satisfying life look like to you today?

Getting to know Jesus Christ more and more as time goes by. The health of my family especially my wife and kids. As well as mine and not taking it for granted for when I feel great.

Application & Reflection

What did you learn today?

I learned what a rich and satisfying life would look like for me today.

How will it affect you?

Keep learning and getting to know Jesus Christ more and more, and not taking certain things for granted such as health/when I'm feeling great (no anxiety).

Storylines: Discover Your Part in the Story

Day 2: Rebuilding

A quick summary of the Bible is this: God's original plan to dwell with mankind, although broken by sin, continues to be his eternal plan. As we reach the end of the story we see that God's plan will be achieved. Revelation 21:3 says,

> I heard a loud shout from the throne, saying, "Look, God's home is now among his people! He will live with them, and they will be his people. God himself will be with them."

God has always wanted to be with us. The very name given to Jesus as Immanuel reveals this to be true. Matthew 1:23 says,

> Look! The virgin will conceive a child! She will give birth to a son, and they will call him Immanuel, which means "God is with us."

Now that we follow Christ and have received new life, the Holy Spirit comes to dwell in us to spiritually transform us.

> Don't you realize that your body is the temple of the Holy Spirit, who lives in you and was given to you by God?

Read 2 Corinthians 5:17. How much has changed since becoming a follower of Jesus?

The old life is gone; a new life has begun

Read Romans 12:1-2. What action does God want from his people?

For us to give our bodies to him. For us not to copy the behavior and customs of this world.

Read Romans 8:28. How does God use life's circumstances?

God causes everything to work together.

Read Romans 8:29-30. This passage describes the process God uses to save us. Write down the steps God takes in our salvation process to draw us close to himself.

He knew us in advance and chose us to be like his son; called us to come to him; by him calling us gave us right standing with him thus/then he gave us his glory.

What events or people did God use to draw you to himself?

God made me cross paths with Pastor James, Author of this book. He also made me go through a rough season that I continue battling but has gotten better with his help.

Application & Reflection

What did you learn today?

For me not to copy the behaviors and customs of this world instead let God transform me into a new person by changing the way I think.

How will it affect you?

I will let God transform me into a new person by letting him change the way I think.

Storylines: Discover Your Part in the Story

Day 3: Judgment

Everyone of us will die. That's a sobering thought. But is there more to it than that? What happens after we die? As we read through the Bible we see that God created us to live forever.

The Bible speaks of our death, resurrection, and judgment. As Hebrews 9:27-28 says,

> *And just as each person is destined to die once and after that comes judgment, so also Christ died once for all time as a sacrifice to take away the sins of many people. He will come again, not to deal with our sins, but to bring salvation to all who are eagerly waiting for him.*

God paints a very different judgment for those who accept his Son, Jesus Christ, and those who reject him. Everyone lives forever somewhere and where you spend eternity is completely dependent upon your decision about Jesus in this life.

According to the Bible, those who have believed in Jesus Christ have received forgiveness for all our sins, while those who have not believed will pay eternally for their sins. Which will it be for you? Did Jesus pay for your sins or will you?

Read Romans 14:10-12. Who will we give an account to of our life?

Each of us will give an account to God.

Read 2 Corinthians 5:10. What will we receive in judgment?

We will each receive whatever we deserve for the good or evil we have done in this earthly body.

Read Luke 16:19-31. Jesus tells a story about two different people with two different destinies. What is most striking to you about this story?

Everyone knows about the Bible. It is up to each individual of whether or not they want to read it during this lifetime to be saved.

Read Revelation 20:11-15. What is the fate of those whose names are not written in the Book of Life?

They will be thrown into the lake of fire.

Read Hebrews 12:22-24. What is the fate of those who have trusted Jesus Christ to save them?

They will go to the city of the living God, Mount Zion.

Application & Reflection

What did you learn today?

Everyone has the choice of whether they read and follow the Bible or not.

How will it affect you?

I will find a way to continue reading the Bible. I will do my best to implement what I learn.

Storylines: Discover Your Part in the Story

Day 4: Justice

Intuitively, most everyone thinks they are a good person. After all, we are certainly better than all of the other "evil" people in the world today. While we certainly all have our rough days, is it right to send basically good people to hell–for all eternity? How could a loving God do that?

The truth is that we are not basically good people in need of a boost in life. According to God's own words we are all bad people in need of forgiveness. God's perfect justice actually requires a fair and honest judgment of our sin.

In speaking about justice, Abraham in Genesis 18:25 asks,

> Surely you wouldn't do such a thing, destroying the righteous along with the wicked. Why, you would be treating the righteous and the wicked exactly the same! Surely you wouldn't do that! Should not the Judge of all the earth do what is right?

God must judge all sin and all have sinned. Only those who have trusted Christ's forgiveness of their sin can stand before God, completely forgiven. This is perfect justice.

Read 1 John 1:8-10. What happens if we claim to have no sin? What happens if we confess our sin?

We are not living in the truth and are calling God a liar; God will forgive our sins and cleanse us from all wickedness.

Read 1 John 3:4-6. What did come to Jesus do?

Jesus came to take away our sins.

Read Proverbs 24:12. Will it be possible to plead ignorance for our sinful actions?

No, God understands all hearts, and he sees us. He guards our souls and he knows we know.

Read Romans 3:10. Is anyone good enough to make it into heaven?

No one is righteous — not even one.

Read Matthew 13:24-30 and 36-43. How does Jesus explain the ultimate end of all mankind? What do the two different groups represent?

The wheat represents the people of the Kingdom who will be saved. The weeds represent the people who belong to the devil who will be thrown in the fire.

Application & Reflection

What did you learn today?

That pleading ignorance will not save us.

How will it affect you?

Keep learning more by reading the bible and reaching out to other followers such as pastor James to grow with Jesus Christ.

Day 5: Heaven

What will Heaven be like? Revelation 21-22 tells us that there will be a new heaven and a new earth. God will recreate and restore what sin has destroyed. There will be a wedding feast. There will be hope once again. There will be no more crying, no more tears, and no more fears. Today we live in the world of paradise lost but one day we will move into the land of paradise restored. In Isaiah 65:17 God says,

> Look! I am creating new heavens and a new earth, and no one will even think about the old ones anymore.

Creation will be restored, we will be restored, and most importantly, our relationship with God will ultimately be restored. We will walk with God in the Garden once again. We will see Jesus face to face because we will be like him. All that has ever kept us from being the people that God desires us to be will be swept away. Our hearts will be free to fully love and experience God. Heaven will truly be "God with us."

Read Revelation 21:1-7. Write down your impressions:

I knew there will be a new earth but what I didn't know was there would be a new heaven as well. Why is that? Is it to make it better?

My biggest impression however, is that God will be living among us. There will be no more death, crying or pain.

Read Revelation 22:1-5. Write down your impressions:

Leaves being used to heal the nations is miraculous. But is this in Heaven or on Earth? As I thought there should not be the need for healing if it were Heaven. The tree of life bearing 12 kinds of fruit. And there will be no more night. God will shine on us for light.

Application & Reflection

What did you learn today?

That God will live among us in Heaven and that there will be no more night either.

How will it affect you?

It will give me the knowledge to be able to share with others.

Conclusion of Week 4: Restoration

Sum up the story of God's work to restore his creation:

He planted eternity in us (hope). God's original plan is to live with us, so he wants us to give our bodies to him. We will all be judged by God on whether we accepted Jesus or rejected him. Only those who have trusted Christ's forgiveness of their sin can stand before God, completely forgiven. Then God will recreate and restore what sin has destroyed. And we will

live with God in heaven,

CONCLUSION

Congratulations! You have walked through the greatest story of all time. It is my prayer that you were able to see all that God did for you and have embraced his love and forgiveness in Jesus Christ.

Sonrise Church exists to make disciples by leading people in a growing relationship with Jesus Christ. We do this the following ways:

1) We CONNECT people in intimacy with God.

2) We GROW people in their faith.

3) We lead people to SERVE others with joy.

4) We equip people to LEAD others along this journey.

In doing these four things we seek to fulfill the great commission of Jesus who said to us in Matthew 28:18-20:

I have been given all authority in heaven and on earth. Therefore, go and make disciples of all the nations, baptizing them in the name of the Father and the Son and the Holy Spirit. Teach these new disciples to obey all the commands I have given you. And be sure of this: I am with you always, even to the end of the age.

Please let us know how we can lead you further in your relationship with Jesus Christ.

James Gleason
Lead Pastor, Sonrise Church

Sonrise Church • 6701 NE Campus Way • Hillsboro, OR 97124
503-640-2449 • www.isonrise.com • office@isonrise.com

Made in the USA
San Bernardino, CA
23 March 2019